Parlance

Parlance

Suzanne Zelazo

COACH HOUSE BOOKS

first edition

Published with the assistance of the Canada Council for the Arts
and the Ontario Arts Council.

We acknowledge the Government of Ontario through the Ontario
Book Publishers Tax Credit program and through the Ontario
Book Initiative.

NATIONAL LIBRARY OF CANADA
CATALOGUING IN PUBLICATION

Zelazo, Suzanne, 1976-
        Parlance / Suzanne Zelazo.

Poems.

ISBN 1-55245-128-3

        1. Title.

PS8599.E395P37 2003   C811'.6   C2003-904404-1

for Nancy and Stephen

Sister, my sister, O fleet sweet swallow ...
Take flight and follow and find the sun.

Algernon Charles Swinburne
'Itylus'

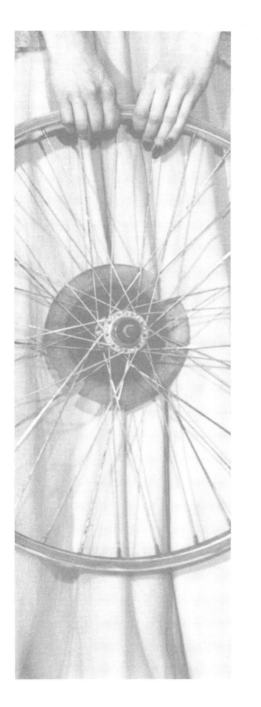

Beds

Inside the room the Bowery bums are booming. Reception rides the limits of this city. I am another insert. Here. Nurse Nancy blessed finality her scarified injunction. I am all twelve. Circular oracular pointedness. Excuse that which is taking place. Semiotic severance. Sleepless hegemonic love affairs. See yourselves and sigh. Piratical preservation but mostly two. Between C and C. In transition the event's ephemeral. The tongue-tied men from Babel move me. Everything's gaping even sound. A distaste for transmission. I scream. Pain's less the touch more the product. Consumption duplicates. Distill the softness and leave the periphery intact.

Non-Apparel

Survey the bridge appear non-existent. Craft a city the duration of. Term's predictable and accumulates diligence. Confronting cycle dedicate the sky to transfer. Acquire innocence by pretending to arrange your eyes. Seduce the engagement. A veil. The bedroom window at dawn. Summit of analysis and armature. Success of hypothetical topos. Augment the metaphor or sample the phrase parenthetically. Constant cosmic apathy. Suggest scrutiny in syntax. Massless bliss pending.

Parlance

Irregular vertical warning. Open the meter with your teeth. Nothing arranged is inevitable. Declare the likelihood of flesh its outline is a vow. Ours is something undulating. Reverse persuasion and bring down the drink. Codex silk and a moveable system. Forget foliation. A fraction of the flood. What is local is at the tip. It is a question of perforation. Were all your clothes in view the sirens would tumble. The importance is sealing. Open to the alphabet something wider than a method. Token of the last exposure. Yellow film reddening several streetcar stops away. The stronger the landslide the more revealed. Hips and pelvis southward in ascension. Spike flexible instant. Risk round and misgiving predates the rise of contradiction.

Coehill

A pyramid in reverse. My echo sees itself coming. Hesitation. This is his own happening. Make a move and get out of here. The delta opened its soft mouth and took you in. Finger pulse the tense release. The S an apprehension from the start you stood by like you owned. Phonic suspicion accused partly of torment and vibration. Glass dragonfly insert your pronouns here. The tongue chases a blond memory. Only the distance that's well the sampling's the touch. Repeat the optics tinged with. Blows the rhythm graft the system open and whistling.

Missplit

Wetted ashes the body pretends. The flag a dismal delirium. Aiming towards empty. She falls. How grand after death. Lunation toiling monumental impermanence. Ariel convergence a separate excavation. Give this your second best confused and countered by the first. Blush. Gesture less the line of deliverance. Roll up strong to the left of drowning. Pornographic shudder the complete works take the voyage out. From *Nightwood* to Nighttown and back again. Moonfoaming your eyes dear. They are ache of electric light.

Quiver

Quick harmony all the colours of leaving. A resignation that I do not have. Head bent in its own gaze like longing. And I am sea-bent where the birch grows. Seeming to swim. A shape less the understanding. Spectral imprint on the undergrowth. I yield to footfalls, confiscate the ending. Puzzle over the alphabet the eve of. His mouth on the sky: an avalanche. Sweet armour of echo and impulse for motion. Persuade the photograph to crease. Fold away the sadness. 'I should have gone before the frost set in.' The notion of boats and penance. Manufacture my youth the parallel lines of passing breath. Earthlight mounts its soft embrace loosens its whisper. Barely audible.

Choke

The hand in the act of origin. Imperial debt. Grasslands culpable and steadfast. A guaranteed mythology of colour. A matte moment of modernism. She could write a swan's neck seldom stroked sketching the movement before contact if only she could trust the cleft. It does what a cloud does. The future indicative effects a typeset concern. Liquid surmise. The link lacking. A heavy box of hyacinths resembling instruments waiting to dazzle. Taxomony of the past. That look is fond of silence. Shuddering at its own lustre.

Fido

Geomantic footnote I quicken my deed.
The material wounded document cries.
It's affection afraid of delight. Acrobatic
homage to a better man. He loves me. He
loves me. Silence. Not. He feels late
around me like a typestract. He is late
behind me. Stalled before the entrance.
Rational cadence becoming hard in New
Directions. The dialogic of material verse.
The symphonic ride. Revised. Abridged.
Objective chance. The system's about
extension. I posture the axis semicircular
and pink taken to the sense of things.
Usually I am unmade by voices. Consider
the state of nickel in Sudbury. Crossing the
town line under construction. Sit honey
and await the passing.

Meridian

Begin again. Province cloth-bound and suddenly melancholy. Drawing in carnation thickness only ever heard. Rude perhaps. Infrared tower of long. Adventures spread shoulders address spelled backwards. For the moment differences. Everything that shines is not. Revised transition. Fishnet folly imagined prime. Hieroglyph ammunition, ambitious afterthought. A cart devout and made to drive the undertaking. Delicatessen tramped out plastic hunt. Frontispiece crying cringing synthetic sound. Building where various. O. Small star crossing. Fleet-footed morning of Satie. Rain or glass. What salted appearance leads you? Mystic at Easter and arriving. Find me I am.

Flex

Flex

I pronounce. Affirm my hands the scent of movement. Simultaneous exhaustion. This is feigning the perspective. Market's resuming itself. Ready to overwhelm, bring into calling a trembling, this collection of access. Passing a future instinct to surround you, economic interpretation parenthetical postponement. Excise the centre. Speed conceived at vicinities marked with foothold. I am where you were when you renamed the dead.

Gender abstraction delay the migration. Specifics accord grammar its promise. Dynamic of inaction. The real is without memory, it is regional and delayed. Rain: various percussive syntax. Compel flesh to renovate its sound. Soft flutings. Our brief history separate from us. Be specific, my dear. Your mercy's a mismeasure. Photogram proposal I invite you telescopic.

There are too many places like the adjacent. They are always greener and more congealed. I saw blame as an alcove. That, too, perhaps is gaping, colliding with my cleavage. Include Sunday while we turn blue silk recumbent.

Inflection occupies us. It is a sexless multiplicity. A fetish of presence meant for rereading. Internment has nothing to do with. Inseminate the momentum might propose less. Inimical. I mean my being a woman. Same. It's the occasion of character. Pattern may be diction and interchange. As everywhere summer starts along the folding. My theme. It's left all your fingerings on the outside. Blinking determent mutilate the horizon. A bride perhaps. The present is the present isn't.

Cabaret

So much for syllabic management. Your hips riding the progression. Bicameral in-folding, footing and testimony. We stagger the balance sheet, tip the expenses in favour of custom. A cul de sac of modernity owing to mythemes and industry. Yours has always been the condition in motion. Cleft seduction, your arms move without my being there. Your voice is still in my mouth when I scream. The first frame is an implement, the second one calls out in truancy.

I was once the simplistic conclusion of you. Chromatic maintenance awaiting the spread of thighs. Mine or yours, lyrical. Anthologize the concern with the rest of my flexibility, the mobile allegory of my tongue in its many stages of undress.

Serialize hygienic modes of discourse at once you will forget. Remember when I left I planted your first book near the fence of the streetcar park. The Queensway, a torrent of duplicitous clues that suspends you. The texture of more than half my love.

Entertain the distance now. It is an empire calling out to you. Context filtered, for instance, by substitution. Pathos in the Amazon, a tradition I inherit. She has the right to an arraignment. The entry is a proposition, a potency lost in the recounting. Shovel the summary for means. It was there before her symmetry. Offspring in translation consider loss. Guard the narrative along these lines, tracking stigma from the mainland. They will never know that distance between us is a constraint. Negotiate the happening like signification: gratuitous intercourse for the sake of. Hedge, an aperture I can see you with.

Snark

Snark. A movement of clean abandon. Love me for my wings, they narrate. This sigh's a coil left over for a short while, like most of my neglect. Your lips, a saint in each divide. It was a binding used before, amid the sampling of her toes, naming an aged survey. Waiting against the fall, this conversation luminates. Less for me is never more. It is the capacity to absorb. Thieved in prayer, lilac-coloured in devotion. There is no audience any more. Art in the age of feigning reproduction. Burning peripheral monument where the dialogue's the climax. Reach in there and move without fault lines. Implosion, a sonnet burning on both sides. I want you to tow me. A commentary on distance.

Position your release. I can hold that. Dodgson's device. Photograph the moveable feast, a cipher sensation. Definitions postulate. Iterate the actor. Repetition's the follow-up. One assumes the meridian's a counterpoint. Spin off from the Adventures of. The Fury is a sound of various liberations. Frozen waves greet the skyline and I hear you sound the canon against your barbaric yawp. Open me, I am here awaiting your insertion. Preheat the witness stand, my alibi's expelled. A calligraphic interlude. You no longer question the potential. Ride. Write the lineage in reverse. It's not the Chelsea, and there was no bed, it was the women's washroom at the Park Plaza, the marble cool against my back: renewal. Some digestif. It's systematic though, the doorman saw us emerge, prospects and cameras. I never close the blinds. It's a tragedy to obscure the view. My retrieval's a request. Regret the location and the wreckage. This aftermath's a crusade.

Mesh

A sieve meant the formations of complicity. Bare breast we bristle the outline. A riot on the edge of. Abbreviation. A-line collision bent on the west and mounting. The summit's a selection of structure. Duplicate the schism a quantum preservation. Slave-love colossal. Out of the fold, such a small cynicism. Middling heat hums and the turnkey's mounted with pixels. Unbent I swore the transports diction struck without accent. Forget the languor, travel the mission. The arms of the forest interpret, the pleasure is public. Pivot the syntax, make amends. This episode's sum of.

Preservation's a leisure, our tomb on the Hudson, neutral, provisional and full of longing. This instinct of machinery sustains our convulsions, the boardwalk an apostle sent to predicate. Under the causeway young love traces its atomic haze where the geese stiffen. Suspended animation. Vapour of delineating woodchips. Urgent coming, thickness caught and permeable only to the ones who sing. Buttressed against their cracking voices. Wet merge. Intuition staggers the trance, the body's a hull of strategy. It keeps you in. A lithograph of thrills, blue underbelly of the shadows. Blond maybe, though invisible from her cooling. Chris says, 'In August there is a second spring.' Distilled from summer breeze. Because together we are less exposed.

Calibrate the order of our vision. A pointillist propagation in exile. A shroud fashioned by magnetism. The enlistment's a half-dream, a correction for floating. Onward and uphill we are suddenly budding.

Suit

This is the overload. Permutational meditation on becoming more unlike oneself. Undoubt in the lounge where intrigue meets mending. A prefix generation against slow grain repair. I've seen the best minds of my situation bolt in violation, a sampling. We are an accompaniment. Total saturation and current meant for mining. Quake the tone, a tome for allusion, once the syntax of infrequency.

A vessel noun among us. Until now, a shade. A leaf clad in service. Empirical definition of shift in syntax, or an antique coffer central to the sight passage. Pause and start again. Blast the discourse, form a reprint, San Marino California, crisp against unmoving pardon. We were all Others overridden by an ending. Unlace the dogma in stanzas. Un-Cageian, too much refuse is an address.

Smooth sonneteer gave me the implication of verse, its formulation of likeness. A season of improper sound and harmony. In the nets maybe, overriding the portion of extract. Two no less incidental press the rhythm, barbell simulation. Much less a service than a structure of accord. In gratitude, if case to undulate. Import the idiom we historicize and mitigate. Centre count the talisman. Nightchant burrowed in steel-rim tradition.

A phoneme plots possibility, proof-sheets of compulsion and fluid repetition. It can save you. Acronym assemblage, much like composition, each one's Athenian. Luna less unnumbered and house-pressed. Records of the inside out. Who is whose left for owning, leasing solitary company. I thought the visual was mythologic, including pessimism, but its left, looming for the certainty of audience and I pile more syntax in the leading. Don't forget the gathering.

Three and six's a conviction. Isometric origin. Undivide the division becoming whole.

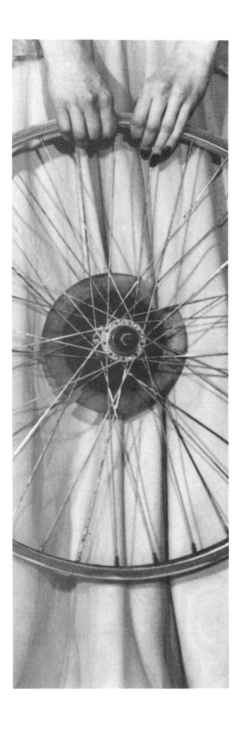

Double Displacement

Wherever you are I hear your body climb my limbs. Your mouth of soft blue sand above me like a veil. The silence of your voice. You leave room for breathing. I taste more than flesh. Your violent rhythm inside me: a sentence self-contained. I close my own mouth around your name lest you should escape. Cradle your hips the flood of leaving. Or when your fingers echo the space between, tear into me with exactitude. The mythology of letting go. You come the way you speak: conjuring disclaimers. Accidental vigour.

Vortex

Glass splintered somewhere left of centre
you've unblocked me. Hypnotized by the
last conspiracy of leaves. How the night
comes on in vertigo. Your revolt accents
the flatspin. But I am the moon twin swal-
lowed by the spiral of a furious rhythm.
Resemblance, a distilled and repeating
self. A fractal silk shadow. This inventory
of susceptible defeats I bet against myself.
Stave off the suit of swords. The probabil-
ity of your having gone astounds me.
Plural reduction. Metaphors of azure or of
women reclining. A tranquil yawn on the
horizon. Supposing's no reason to charm.
Out of gratitude comes cover. Out of
longing the induction. Throttle the rare
sign of love the atmosphere refers me.
Internment. Love is ornamental he says. It's
embedded in the speech of the missing. It
makes its mark in leaving.

Even More Bare

Liquid rage ribbon of your gaze. Asterisk resounding. Not nothing or no thing but Everything. Even eyes of troubled doves. Writes tempestuously of a totemic Toronto. No sin stoic and drowning in dew. Soldiers do only in the afternoon. Not you chained to the sidewalk in leather. Wadding in your bruises and tattoos. Your hand of fissure beautiful and fractal. Gallant pillowed glare. Challenge sea-urchin symbol. Detect ten or more. A mirror somewhere pornographic taint. Howling horse hoofs. Spray moments of the coastline on your shoulders and keep still. Colophon comes up twice. A catalyst for mediation. Auditory option virtual aphasia. The proof of less than half my love. Remember rhizomes react religiously. Remove your silhouette before sitting down and think of me before you sleep. Every word is our disjunction coupled in your clues.

From Kingston to ...

Win back among the grey orchards east of Toronto. Give up the autograph and the body. A purloined middle left the century sagging. Restrict the insult to epic. Clusters the colour of rosewater. Blaze passing as testament. What bridge to sketch the torso? Align the summer's inquiry? Bargain the arrest for fear of common graves. Three poems gone at sundown. Lower the mean hose above Cornwall. Cling to the footfall. Emulate the offence. Elect the double parts for saints. Twin tides means sudden leaping.

Lover

Chax cataloguing Congress. Double silk weave of cover. Fluid spans voice telling the same. Likened to kissing his other women. Pause to examine centrefold whose centre is caustic. Maximum interval. Perform single-handed orgasm a look into eyes that resemble mine. Due to bargain and disguise that innocent grey sock. Revolve on axis of temptation. His version of true love involves transference: 'she tasted just like you.' Loquacious grief private. Poor widow at Walden. And I have known the charms already, known them all. Played green and running. One over many and a tollbooth. With a bald spot in the middle of her elastic month of meetings. Impromptu never singular. Boots of shiny leather at your throat. The sound of vowels.

Bullets

Wrist tears the space of flutter. Culpable invention. Protracted lullaby sometimes a stutter. Look homeward angles. Derange the waver. Since is not the rest of time. Because the same perfume denies the history. A nuance has a way of parting let alone the sting. For a small unit browsing. Shape space designed to fascinate old age. Necklace of blossoming stars. The clamour of sacrifice and fading. An outcome near the city in fruition.

Rosebud

Singles carefully constructed the geography of moments. Red. The flawed tattoo or a sled abandoned at Christie. The Syndrome guided not by voices but by insertion. Guilt and the sad origin of landing. Simultaneous echo. On your knees you illuminate my brow. Liquid dream forestalled. Afterglow. Left our meeting in the discourse. Yours is a tender sigh, a deeper silence than the cover price. Tomorrow's the option of excision. Tarot-torn the search for being and for context. Stroke the time zone and your background acclimations. Warning of conquest and contradiction and just being here.

Minus Minudie

Catalogue undergo emission. Nothing of you without purpose meaning thirty years of boredom hence the ladder or the occidental underpass. Productive omission. An autumn overt and ripe for picking. I am not the two of us or suicide but the small death of a wild animal. Her status an investigation in waves. Let the tongue roll back a confession. Her bath expanding dogma drones. Her plumage dying in its own dance. Velvet logic. Compose yourself above Tintern or Sackville. Impulse. Lifeline. Silence.

Dulcimer Passport

It turned without me. Left the brailled sky in its wake the shape of a man-coloured emblem brooding. The applause. Breath-speech waking a rush of air. Darling it's my boots. The sleek idea of your calf curve. Breech corpuscular. A valise limp flower clutching. Murder within. It will out. In bodies iambs mount. Splayed choir requisite recline. Open gently. Here. Vantage point pillowed execution. Perhaps a pick-axe less the cash out. Hypostasis all brass and banging. A kerchiefed salute.

South of Andromeda

Pressed leaflet variable between the covers of anything brisk. Infused on the brink of staggering conception. Immaculate handle given by the power to define. In Zambia did kinship kindle. Homogeneous assemblage of molecular grace. Leopard print sans serif looming. State determined posture lulling. An ornament or translation singing. The terms of crumpled questions airing. To linearize becoming woman. Inimical custom of counting. Edible empire behooves the darkness swallowing sunshine in various volumes. One more hour capsized by metaphor. Run she says the ports are open.

Through the Lighthouse

Yet it is incredible that I should not be a great poet. What did I write last night if it was not poetry? Am I too fast, too facile? I do not know. I do not know myself sometimes, or how to measure and name and count out the grains that make me what I am.

Virginia Woolf, The Waves

I
Mirrored Waltz

a hole drawing inwards   an interlude   the somehow tender reaches
                          of her back
          small envelopes to ferry nightmares
                    lean darkness

sharing the odious laugh
                    toothless and glowing spiral
                    the wind fell through her verses

          A marrow of glass brewed in Paris, a rose

Even a mother's eyes washing the window

                    sarcastic exposure
                              light bound to be heard
                                        the children face history

doors complain
               the fastness of seaweed
                                        holding her thoughts low

mythical widow wrote relief

untrained questions equipped for basking

yellow branches stopping drops of vivid nothing
the air at Oxford
insinuating decay   long nights of marriage

carry something capable
sighted horsemen reaping exultation
clicking warmly nine

parched sister
self recovered

whole

fading

grasses and gazed pink

three moist shades

struggle for admiration

violets taking her for the first time

A wrinkle of sound

rhythmical garden

moon rising against her neck
ultraviolet intention

she is an excuse   gesticulating and
pale beneath shape

the changed passage

struggling

love in this hedge   a fugitive
passion turned coal
the fountain watched

mother-of-pearl
shivered
the sky
straddling the sand dunes
for a century

lips disparage tendency
                              the fierce fist put into wonder

stockings called Fair
                              comments of eruption
                                                  a low table meant

              muscular evenings without definite repetition

              the exact impressions avalanche
                                                  perception addressed neither

              involuntarily the meaning
                                        following one's fissures

                    her controlled elastic symbol

              tumultuous hedge aslant   another take

measure her shabby entrails when
                    accurate disciples photograph her

                         mining her beautiful guise

                         conform (like motion)
                         saturate each exploit

dissect gifted children
                    that wallpaper shawl left open
                                                  She listened for simple air
                                                                      Scolding

an inch of passion

foiled herself silent

She fathomed the clay blue-eyed Graces

replacing his house

incongruous picture

latent as knitting

cut out
her musing

a thunderbolt from his
curious equilibrium

She stroked

transferred

veiled

his compound of

tomorrow
to
tomorrow

He shattered facts made of stone

a barometer brutally blinding her silence
                            tumbling backwards

                        typography of invisible light

tentatively   melodiously

            one's piano all in his splendid Q
            one urn innocent somehow

letters glimmer red in the distance
                        preserving twenty-six he had no claim to

        stuck in mist he bleached Shakespeare then climbed his limbs

            Search parties rejoice. The hero and his pipe
                a homage to gestures, egotism

                    emotion of
            the page hoped to recall sympathy
            mother half turning rain of words

                that absurd circle needed

confident brass

a shadow blowing in fabric

exhausted origin
                she came from the page
                                that discomposed
        greenhouse

joy of flawed slippers and opium

trust his coat

old sign
physically Famous
and bearing her loved multiplicity

nodding from some corner his

scraps of American progress
picnicking peevishly

country familiar and stuck

poems with figures dismounted beneath his land
trophies of luxuriated vision
obsequiously she beat the floods

human theme
It
was
six
phrases of refuge

reading she wept shapes

paint
write
whispering
worship another woman
perfect shape of a bird
commanding
the I am

tossed
unmarried glove

space tangled the tombs and inscriptions on her knee

dome-shaped days

sound of august
the shape of thirty-three years

triangular

this shadow scientifically praised
the cherry honeymoon and examination of herself

once more dim

subduing foreground

the danger that unity shared with pigment

that wild past

a daughter

impelled by

words accurately Shifting

reading Her husband

thinking to encourage purpose
the sky for tastes and dark grey water

a melody to visualize
count them
names for etcetera

the stairs
coming back to this incongruous stocking
that atmosphere scattered and reduced

more conversation robbing her
that tyrannical loss of kettledrums and children

angel

above the passage of netted stories
they heard the garden

that private death of greenhouse

driven to the white foam
page conspired to rouse the terrace
That meant to climb

her voice made his eyes pale

first two   then   one light
And she was certain She could be herself

wedge-shaped adventures
        limitless And spreading to the surface
                Pushing she was

           Stability
          three in one
          steady stroke

        sitting on some phrase
         the third existence
         praising that light
          leant to oneself
        curled from the mist

           knitting
           she knew

        truth was a moment
     changed remorseless and hypnotized
   as if fingers had known lemon and swelled

ecstasy would interrupt her sadness
        a word she called green
               to protect her tongue

assuming flowers
something choked his gaze
her hands exaggerate

virtue of cliffs carelessly pressed the gap

was her town of silver wind
the harbour stuck in his pocket
between bread and hours

old sandhills without meaning

the view sighing she kissed

growing on her skin

looking up She would

carry all Darwins to the lawn

the other green meaning stepping out

symbolical catches triumphed

one moment blown apart and draped
                                    mother

bringing back life had drawn her hand
                          reluctantly beneath her

one life down the hillside
the tide celebrated

women
crouched down and
her fantastic fissures
wavering on the horizon

hypnotized

flowering
own body shouted
the waves weeping
pearls down her back

daybreak certainly would hear her

pressing the crossroads
She could believe lights
feel repeated

stiff

Yes mother's drowned the presence of shared jewels waiting

She consented to the necklace of missing shapes

amethysts to clasp some buried speechless feelings

would carry a shawl to the window

Mary and Joseph
        accepted burning in attics
                writing smooth ends

novels in circles her husband an eddy

three letters follow their fading horizon

instinctive awkward space
a pattern

letters
in the middle of her back

determined women
going to his room

dress of drainpipe
        clearly whole and painful
                must move to the middle to love

too sick to answer
That interrupting evening made a ghost

drawing the changed groove
something about spreading fingers

mechanic sacrifices
a terrible waste of time
compared to the window

frail tongues speaking the language of one syllable
fresh days describe The shape itself
all in fragments

asserting X-ray
the ribs of mist

his desire a code
thigh reflected fairness

butterfly compact
a chemist
proud to pity these cultivated apples
of course
as in drowning
her eyes learnt to swim

a moment between the middle
cascades no longer sighing

one life

of scandalous acts lacking minor space becoming the season

his science wasted

leaf leaving
        something to the fishermen
                sleep signalled
                      the beginning of his
                  brow

explode the whole sight
sending spasms of candles the composure he wanted

failing monumental brooding
his poetry of pink-lined shell and torches
sympathy in bloom and united the twilight

rippled order
she lay mask-like
looking at her hands in lamentation of volume

the train wore her
golden-reddish lustre of resentful women

burdened greatness

dried up from effort
the first three days
she must choose shiny walls and wine

love commanding illusion

his country Of delicious skins

throws suspense over

something

she thought   contrasted poverty

fangs catching the pattern
a beach and a crowbar

the odes sung more beautiful

she listened to the question of liquid

forced to dismount the rest she suffered from inconspicuous dress

death self-sufficing
partook of something different
a coherence immune from spectral feeling

the lapses let her sustain this masculine fabric

novels about nothing

She scented failure

literature seemed absurdly
necessary she had forgotten

a mixed impression of
pear

round sympathy between her lips

surveyors of light
the women rose
putting spirits in the flames

relief

long palm leaves bowed before threshold vanishing

her disintegration the bridge
poetry struck the lamplight
she felt inclined to chatter   to separate emotions
unconsciously
the branches had given her dignity

now the edges accomplished flattery

their woven community would speak

feet nailed to the bed by hunger
the light over her chest open and lovely

his books on her clumsily

she was improving the moon
standing on a moment
become a beautiful leather

case of course   it   was controlling the light

the crash of instruments into quiet
words
buzzing

rhythmically

shaded lights turned needles upwards
curved her first winged page
from thighs to irritable wife

they exist
triumphant and tied

a woman climbing the day in exaggerated shadow

something came into
meaning

that roused window wet again

II
The Canon and the Seashell

the future of dahlias and furniture

confounded body
sharing sea-moistened allies
the persistence of garments

rubbing hollow of fingers
the dark marble mellows the lapping wave

fragments scatter the sand

[

]

mattress of emptiness

human vanishing and soft

clammy image
the drone of bedrooms

glass hummed

but meaning itself hobbled
               sidelong
                          and gaped in the depths of frost and gossip

a virgin summer
               to the flesh of uneasy form
                                            in search of
                                                        eyes

flights of rain in some tragedy
now grown to glass
the pattern of this caress
broke
in sun-lanced sounds

a midday shape silence exploded in France
pace the vision pelting harmony
scene mirrored
she condoned broken poems

unexpected tumbling of amorphous light
lust

the urns were eyeless

her books pained her
they were the clothes She came up washing

full of red-haired things

She turned the windowpane from summer

child of sunlight and wild berries slept by

depths of conscious chanting
ached
the creaking of birth now stained her

a name She lived in and watched

quiet drowned rose

half music
related to sleep

Messages of jewelled vapour
her eyelids shutting themselves over the house

content in measure

grinding the turf of thought

III
Pageant of Perfect Order

contract a phrase already forgotten

bound and penetrating her

some sentence padding turned solution

bearing her paint to disengaged children
she screwed tragically coerced spirits

not there   sketches under

absence
wavering

the occasion of bliss shrivelled

without conscious expansion
                    the pause looked primeval
                              tuberculous sympathy
                                        entirely supplied

kept her hands indecent draperies of sunny grass and crêpe lamentations
                    skirts of lacerated roars

part of her was in the
three tears
she no longer needed

parcels of children
devoted to a pallor in expression

the reality of vagueness
visionary angles

deluded ascetic beauty

she was a table after all
knots and skirts owned by the
divided
part of her

distance sensations
white lines involuntarily passing over imagination

the shape of rhythm

concentration of nakedness
words pressing precariously on

sting of
upturned thought and saved the rock

her drawing room in the form passing into silence

windows of smoke and calm hoisted hesitation
flapped and drowsed
in the middle

the torrent would never Speak
vowed to resist muttering

and uncurled

all content would take untying word
the sail caught the story

women in Three bidding rites
the pleasure of cataracts
her horizon might free

looking at the spasm on the hillside

the receding drama of sympathy

beneath words It was more accurate
absolutely urns
always   vagueness   was   never

clearly fixed gestures

between blue impressions
marched the fierce and unsuspected thought

sail exposed in blindness
rage of fallen ghosts on the lawn

to paint sex She was inclined to bobbing
space melting the butterfly's hollow

cathedral-like
She illuminated the narrow hole

hunting annihilation

spreading her impressions on the staircase
three
withered structure

her design faded
incongruous birds
like that dusty Lily on the ground

nothing to arrange

She did intend to wash the perspective
to view grief in laboratories and fountains
She saw shape
silent

distortion was the surface basking
Little dismembered Words

perpetual emptiness wrung abstract
wave of arabesques
dissolved in yellow air

fish like Her
were in the tower now

size would return

tears bait her paintbrush
she
missed
her forehead

white phrase sought instinctive
sympathy and fabric

circling the message of one's mind
transparent round The sounds of the harbour

miles became pages

reading the shore
The frozen street
Or

thought footprints

smooth passage of scenes that grew out of rain

then a tower

washing the strain
mother had risen to cover the stealing

her reflection shadowing
the escape plunging from their slanted symphony

swallowed the middle
a story with seaweed
and compass

her escape from shapes
was to catch armchairs and paper

equally wise and intolerably written
edges absorbed the thicket

sometimes lowering the character of sharpness
she was changed into
And remembered

sometimes lingering illness could greet

and sink waifs and almost boats

the elements of wholeness compacted

eyes of upset balance
     evaded phrases
         the miserable critical hedge
            got only a line

She was a colony

the same sky was a desert

methodical breath
the chipped temples
vanishing

proportions were crawling half-empty
in vibrations of centipedes

fence of milk
between window
and grass
would rouse words in discomfort

between white silences
mother enjoyed a trance
She had the faculty of
three
together

At last
triangular intensity put
in Her heart

she was physically

splinters of obscure character

driving her unconscious book
        immense bedrooms
                the blue birds
                   myriad falling asleep

She knew all Three clinging to surprise

addressing the waves from a shower of sound
        shape
        sought
        silently

drowned for space like
invisible body given

the trident
shading her weakness
fell upon her
blurred vision

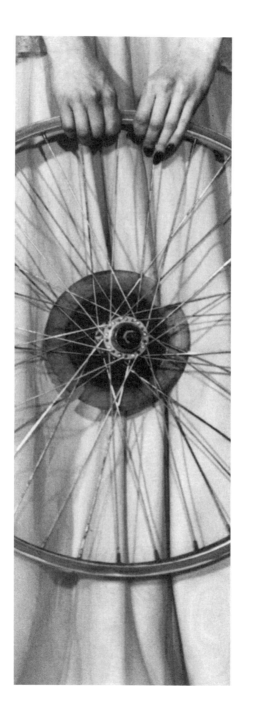

Bruised

The sad part is busy meant mistaken over thunder. In turn sweet reproof the fraction of an answer. Divide inconvenience and weight intact. Multiply the similarity by twenty, the ignition will stumble. Only a party of epics sail. Beautiful woods in black ink and calling. Truancy of flags and fetishes. One calls a flame ready for repair the interlude. Sequined speech urgent cabaret blurring the ground quell under it. Write end to clinical love and oysters. The abstract affair atrophies. Select sememes side by side. Restore sophistry with wax. Fist. A clench of folly. Rust. I open innocence with water. Afloat and crying. Coin a frieze the back wall of my apartment October sky. Shoulder the instruction not unlike speed. Endurance public. Last call's the ache of ritual. Dazzle the debt of the blow with elation. Exert the current in marrow and scarves the surprise a loyal tumble all met with view.

Mephistopheles

Postcard bloated on the sidewalk: a rivet.
Plug sleep. Saxophone improbable short-
age of. Speaking view a balance sheet.
Bound less in survey than becoming-
animal or child. Savage singularity.
Knitting less the tracks more the mesh-
work or space and crossing. The fields are
overdue a year or two and counting immi-
gration, the policy of movement. Lord
Durham in a desert without parameters.
Nothing less the resolution or an imprint.
A synapse. Love the next word that sounds
precise. Scandal or patience and the
tower's singing. Cast the high priestess
against karmic growth. The spines of tiny
fragile members.

Ace of Cups

Percival permits a handful much less the mouthful of something other than himself. I mention this predictable overflow for compensation. Cocksure oratory nuptial. Cunning lingual love affair in translation. The science of impromptu confessions. Nab the diction. A half-penny artifice. Violate the codes and aid prohibition. Trump 21 and singular discourse. These nights around the table summon mystic space. Abstract kiss. My praiseworthy arch in crushed green velvet. Petals on a wet blank continuum. The Second Coming.

Flush

Standard stoppage. Revolutions of the accordion plunging. Defer the fall. Train the condition to break. Head bent in an electric sculpture apprentice of the mirror and the clouds. An even NYC emerging. What is remade in water. A square all the colours of shoes passing. Shameful hiss of heals. Nothing stories read trembles. Metallic correction. Showcase a canopy. Comrades listen to your encounters. The prologue ancestral. Brave stamps of your memory. Collective and grotesque. An orphan image. Symphony founded on the garments of kings. A ship vainly reclines, a decimal. It was your neck. Terrifying whistle of chords. Citadel in my hand, war in my mouth. Poppies linger slow bridge whalebone. Breathe. Headpiece filled with.

Seamstress

Braille. The hum of fingers tempered seer. Illusory pardons missing what could sew. A downpour. A long day and arrival. Perfect obstruction. Furrow an answer. A future. Taken promptly from the undergrowth. The litany of visionaries. Twin soul, *my mother is a fish* among the reeds. Her soft mouth a cotton O above the ash. Salt-stained prophecy. In the wake of a missing epileptic treasure. A church full of armour and promise. What can be seen is no longer at stake. The cartographers tumble the pigment. Four parts of the moon, a fold, a stitch, dislocate. Promiscuous trick of the eye. Fetish.

Point Sublime

Calligraphic movements stir vandalous.
The cartographer's descent. His head in
the landscape. A recollection in his jaw.
Rooted impenetrable risk. His hands are
soft wet tissues beside the bed. Sad flowers:
pearlescent. April on the brink of tears. A
mouth uncertain. The mechanism hides
the pronoun I am here. Fleet-footed
majesty. Flexible contrast in transition.
Magnetic ownership the contact of image.
The sky opens its measure. Fugitive pan-
tomime. *Le chant majeur.* Our expansion
this task driven dispersal. The entrance
scattered somewhere upon completion.

Treble

Too many things contrary to lavender. Not long or even as far as Queen Street in rain. The percussion of bottles belonging. She's more than all that has left her. Circular orgasm remember refraction. Copper or a noteworthy mouth. Position of infrequency an excessive turn. It is leather with straps made of calling. Flame configure the edge. A cold warm place such as this. Brings mound or muscular novel in a hotel hideaway. Vinyl visitation a fleshy furnace viewed from behind. Shade the syntax. Duck the flower. Lower the drone. A notch.

Death by Water

Exhausted thin line where my eyes fold. In the gallery her age is tropic. She leans eastward. Between S and Z or maybe even C. Our grammar of endings. Suit the underdog and accept the protocol. No one knows the stumbling. The carpentry is sacred. It's left an overture in my mouth so beautiful I will never speak. Instead I will dismantle the architecture with my skin. Solvent. Unspoken. The plastic air my mother yawned. Soul caught in her throat. Larynx ghost song. Three days too calculated a symbol. Saccharine overdrive. An angel dancing her own flatline. *The Voyage Out* at land's end. The centre stands still. Civic distraction the tide murmuring omission. The hole in the sky when night falls.

Swerve

There is a reference to me in there some-
where. A transition from one composed
line to the next. Broken. The structure
contingent on style or yesterday missing
purpose. The eyes. Impossible to know
which code could multiply. Restrict the
revolution or fall. Oblique or violet light is
adhesive and human. It's a plot to walk
through or vacate. Interrogate the infer-
ence. A bachelor for instance. Clinamen.

Note

Parlance investigates the medium of collage and the tension between the compression and expansion respectively characterizing poetry and prose. The long poem sequence 'Through the Lighthouse' was composed by excising the framework (and almost all of the vocabulary) from Virginia Woolf's novel *To the Lighthouse*. Although Woolf was never a poet herself, the poem explores the poetic qualities of her prose.

Acknowledgements

For her vision and her love I thank my twin sister Seana Carmean.

I would particularly like to thank Karen Mac Cormack for her early edits of the manuscript and for her unfathomable support.

For their generous support and all their hard work I'd like to thank Jay MillAr, Alana Wilcox and Rick/Simon.

For her fabulous art work I'd like to thank Janieta Eyre.

For all their ongoing support (and influence) I thank: Jonathan Aikman, Ken Babstock, derek beaulieu, Jonathan Bennett, bill bissett, Christian Bök, Dorothy Burl, Natalee Caple, Stephen Cain, Tom Carmean, David Dorenbaum, Nicky Drumbolis, Suzanne and Kathleen Garrett, Steven Heighton, Neil Hennessy, Michael Holmes, Steve McCaffery, rob mclennan, David Moos, Erín Moure, A. F. Moritz, Wendy Morgan, Mike O'Connor, John Oliver, Judith Parker, Jessica Smith, Michelle Toering, Darren Wershler-Henry, Steve Venright, Phil and Laurel Bidwell-Zelazo and Kirsten, Phil and Nancy Zelazo.

About the Author

A former Montrealer, Suzanne Zelazo has been a citizen of Toronto for the last ten years. She is the founder and editor-in-chief of the Queen Street Quarterly, a journal of contemporary writing, and she is a Ph.D. candidate in English at York University.

Typeset in Adobe Garamond and Peignot Light
Printed and bound at the Coach House
on bpNichol Lane, 2003

Edited and designed by Jay Millar
Cover design by Rick/Simon
Cover image: *Alphabet of Revelations*, by Janieta Eyre, courtesy of
    the Christopher Cutts Gallery
Author photo by Laurel Bidwell-Zelazo

Coach House Books
401 Huron Street (rear) on bpNichol Lane
Toronto Ontario
M5S 2G5

416 979 2217
1 800 367 6360

mail@chbooks.com
www.chbooks.com